Renewing The Mind

Unlocking the Mind of Christ

TOM CORNELL

CONTENTS

INTRODUCTION
THE BATTLE FOR THE MIND AND THE POWER OF RENEWAL

The greatest battle in life is not fought in the realm of the physical but in the realm of the mind. What we think determines how we live, how we perceive God, and how we respond to the world around us. The mind is the control center of our life, shaping our beliefs, emotions, and decisions. It is the lens through which we interpret everything we experience. The enemy knows this well, which is why his primary attack is on our thoughts. If he can shape how we think, he can control how we live.

However, God has called us to a higher way of thinking—a Kingdom way of thinking. Scripture tells us that we are not to be conformed to this world but to be transformed by the renewing of our minds (Romans 12:2). This is not just an encouragement to think positively or adjust our perspective—it is a call to think with the mind of Christ (1 Corinthians 2:16). We are no longer bound by the limitations of natural reasoning, fear, or deception. As sons and daughters of God, we are called to think like our Father, align with His will, and manifest His Kingdom on Earth.

This book is about stepping into that transformation. It is

about renewing your mind so that you no longer think like the world, like your past, or like the enemy—but like God. When you align your thoughts with Heaven, your life shifts. You begin to see the impossible as possible, fear is replaced with faith, and confusion gives way to divine clarity. The renewed mind doesn't just lead to better decisions—it leads to supernatural living.

The Mind: The Gatekeeper of Your Life

Everything in life flows from the way we think. The mind is a gatekeeper—it either opens the door to the realities of the Kingdom of God or locks us into the limitations of the natural world.

Proverbs 23:7 says, *"As a man thinks in his heart, so is he."* This means that the way you think determines the way you live. Your perspective shapes your reality. If you see yourself as weak, you will live in defeat. If you see God as distant, you will struggle to experience His presence. If you believe lies, you will walk in bondage. But if you align your mind with the truth, you will walk in freedom, authority, and supernatural power.

The Bible is filled with examples of people who were transformed because their thinking was changed. Moses went from seeing himself as an inadequate stutterer to becoming a deliverer of a nation. Gideon saw himself as weak and insignificant until God showed him that he was a mighty warrior. Peter went from denying Jesus in fear to boldly proclaiming the gospel with power. What changed? Their minds were renewed to see themselves through Heaven's perspective.

In contrast, we also see the devastating effects of a carnal and unrenewed mind. The Israelites, though chosen by God, wandered in the wilderness for 40 years—not because God had abandoned them, but because their minds were still enslaved.

They saw themselves as grasshoppers, unable to possess what God had already given them (Numbers 13:33). Their old mindset kept them from entering the fullness of God's promise.

The same is true today. God has already prepared incredible things for those who love Him (1 Corinthians 2:9). He has called us to walk in power, joy, and victory. But the question is, can we perceive it?

The Spirit of God Reveals the Mind of God

The world operates from a limited mindset, relying only on human logic, past experiences, and natural understanding. But as believers, we have been given the Spirit of God, who reveals to us the deep things of God. Paul writes in 1 Corinthians 2:9-12, 16:

"Eye has not seen, nor ear heard, nor have entered into the heart of man the things which God has prepared for those who love Him. But God has revealed them to us through His Spirit. For the Spirit searches all things, yes, the deep things of God. For what man knows the things of a man except the spirit of the man which is in him? Even so no one knows the things of God except the Spirit of God. Now we have received, not the spirit of the world, but the Spirit who is from God, that we might know the things that have been freely given to us by God... For 'who has known the mind of the Lord that he may instruct Him?' But we have the mind of Christ." NKJV

This passage is life-changing. It tells us that we are not limited to natural understanding—we have access to the very mind of Christ through the Spirit of God. The things that once seemed hidden are now revealed to us. We no longer have to guess what God is thinking—we can know His thoughts.

The renewed mind is a mind in agreement with God. Amos

3:3 says, "Can two walk together unless they are agreed?" Many people live their lives trying to get God to agree with them, but God will not change His mind to walk with us—we must change our thinking to walk with Him.

This is why the renewal of the mind is so essential. It is not just about thinking more positively or changing a few behaviors —it is about coming into agreement with how God thinks, sees, and operates.

The Role of Sonship in Renewing the Mind

When we are born again, we are not just forgiven—we are adopted as sons and daughters of God. In Hebrew, the word for son is ben, which means "builder of the Father's house." This means that as sons, we don't just receive an inheritance—we are called to partner with the Father in expanding His Kingdom.

Jesus did not come only to reveal the Father—He came to show us what it means to be a son. In John 5:19, Jesus said,

"The Son can do nothing of Himself, but what He sees the Father do; for whatever He does, the Son also does in like manner." NKJV

This is how we are meant to think and live. A renewed mind is one that sees what the Father is doing and moves in alignment with it. Jesus is the perfect model of sonship. He walked in absolute unity with the Father, always thinking, speaking, and acting in agreement with Heaven. This is the standard for us. A renewed mind understands:

- We are sons, not orphans. Orphans beg, but sons inherit.
- We are builders, not consumers. Sons are entrusted with the Father's business.

- We are imitators of God. Sons reflect their Father's nature.
- We are not victims of circumstance. Sons operate from Heaven's reality.

When we truly grasp who we are and whose we are, our thinking shifts. We no longer think like slaves, but like sons. We no longer strive for what God has already given—we walk in it with confidence.

What This Book Will Teach You

This book is designed to take you on a journey of mind renewal. You will learn:

- How to shift from carnal thinking to Kingdom thinking
- How to align your thoughts with Heaven's reality
- How to break free from strongholds and deception
- How to think with the mind of Christ and operate in supernatural wisdom
- How to walk in agreement with God and manifest His will on Earth

This is not just about learning new information—it is about experiencing radical transformation.

As you read, I encourage you to invite the Holy Spirit to renew your thinking, expand your faith, and align your mind with the Father's. You were made to think like Jesus, live in victory, and see the Kingdom of God manifest in your life.

The journey begins now.

CHAPTER 1

THE POWER OF RIGHT THINKING

THOUGHTS SHAPE REALITY

The greatest battles we face in life are not external but internal. What we think determines how we live. Everything we experience, believe, and do is shaped by the way we think. Before any significant decision, action, or transformation happens in our lives, it first begins as a thought.

Proverbs 23:7 declares, *"As a man thinks in his heart, so is he."* This simple yet profound statement reveals that we are the product of our thoughts. If we think in defeat, we will live defeated. If we think in fear, we will live bound by fear. But if we think in alignment with God's truth, we will live in the fullness of His promises.

The battle for right thinking is not new. From the very beginning, Satan has sought to influence the way people think. The mind is the enemy's primary battlefield. He knows that if he can control your thinking, he can control your life. He doesn't have to physically overpower you if he can get you to agree with a lie.

The Garden War: How the Enemy Attacks the Mind

The first battle in human history wasn't fought with weapons

—it was fought with words, ideas, and deception. In Genesis 3, the serpent approached Eve and said:

"Has God indeed said, 'You shall not eat of every tree of the garden'?" -
Genesis 3:1 NKJV

Notice how the enemy didn't attack Eve with force—he attacked her with an idea. He planted a question that challenged what she knew to be true. His strategy was not to overpower her but to influence her thinking.

This is the same tactic the enemy uses today. He whispers thoughts of doubt, confusion, and fear, making us question:

- "Did God really say He will provide?"
- "Are you sure you're truly forgiven?"
- "What if God isn't really good?"
- "Maybe you're not worthy of His love."

These thoughts, if left unchecked, can shape how we see God, ourselves, and our purpose. The enemy's goal is not just to plant doubt but to get us to agree with lies. Because once we believe a lie, we begin to live in its reality.

The fall of man was not just about eating a forbidden fruit—it was about agreeing with a false perspective of God. Eve accepted a distorted idea that God was withholding something good from her. This wrong belief led to wrong action.

This pattern is still true today:

- What we believe determines how we behave.
- What we think shapes how we live.
- Every victory or defeat begins in the mind.

This is why renewing the mind is the key to transformation.

Renewing the Mind: Thinking Like Sons, Not Slaves

Romans 12:2 is one of the most powerful scriptures about the importance of right thinking:

> *"Do not be conformed to this world, but be transformed by the renewing of your mind, that you may prove what is that good and acceptable and perfect will of God."* NKJV

The command here is clear:

1. Do not conform – Don't think like the world.
2. Be transformed – Change happens when the mind is renewed.
3. Prove God's will – Right thinking leads to clarity of purpose.

The renewed mind is the gateway to transformation. It is impossible to live a victorious life while thinking like a slave.

Israel's journey from Egypt to the Promised Land is a perfect example of how wrong thinking can keep us from God's best. Though the Israelites were freed from slavery, their minds were still bound by a slave mentality.

When they faced challenges, they complained and wished to return to Egypt (Numbers 14:3-4). Even though they were physically free, they still thought like slaves. Their un-renewed minds caused them to:

- Doubt God's promises
- See obstacles as impossible
- Live in fear rather than faith

Because of this mindset, an entire generation missed out on the Promised Land. Their way of thinking kept them from stepping into what God had already prepared for them.

This is why the renewed mind is not just about positive thinking—it is about thinking as a son of God.

We Have the Mind of Christ

1 Corinthians 2:9-12, 16 reveals an incredible truth:

"Eye has not seen, nor ear heard, nor have entered into the heart of man the things which God has prepared for those who love Him. But God has revealed them to us through His Spirit… Now we have received, not the spirit of the world, but the Spirit who is from God, that we might know the things that have been freely given to us by God… But we have the mind of Christ." NKJV

This means that we are not left to figure things out on our own. We have access to the thoughts of God through the Holy Spirit. The Spirit searches the deep things of God and reveals them to us.

- The natural mind sees problems; the mind of Christ sees solutions.
- The natural mind fears lack; the mind of Christ trusts in supernatural provision.
- The natural mind operates in self-preservation; the mind of Christ operates in faith and boldness.

When we renew our minds, we stop living from a worldly perspective and start living from Heaven's reality.

Agreement With God: The Key to Transformation

Amos 3:3 says, *"Can two walk together unless they are agreed?"*
NKJV

Many people struggle in their walk with God because they are trying to get God to agree with them rather than aligning themselves with Him. But God will not change His mind to walk with us—we must change our thinking to walk with Him.

The renewed mind is not just about gaining knowledge—it's about coming into agreement with God's perspective. When we agree with God, we:

- See ourselves as He sees us.
- Think with the faith of Heaven.
- Operate in Kingdom authority.

This is why renewing the mind is a daily process. Every day, we are bombarded with messages from the world, the enemy, and our past experiences that try to shape how we think. But we have the responsibility to bring every thought into obedience to Christ (2 Corinthians 10:5).

Activating the Renewed Mind: Practical Steps

1. Immerse Yourself in God's Word

- The Word of God is the foundation for renewed thinking.
- Meditate on the truth (Joshua 1:8) and allow it to shape your thoughts.

2. Replace Lies with Truth

- Identify areas where you have been thinking contrary to God's Word.

- Speak the truth over yourself and reject deception.

3. Partner with the Holy Spirit

- The Spirit reveals the mind of Christ—ask Him to teach you how to think like Jesus.
- Spend time in prayer and worship, allowing God's presence to renew your thinking.

4. Refuse to Entertain Toxic Thoughts

- Don't let fear, doubt, or negativity control your mind.
- Take every thought captive (2 Corinthians 10:5).

5. Live in Agreement with God

- God won't change His mind to walk with us—we must align our thinking with Him.
- Choose daily to think, speak, and act according to His truth.

The Invitation to Think Like God

God has so much more prepared for us than we can naturally comprehend (1 Corinthians 2:9). But it is only through a renewed mind that we can step into all that He has freely given us.

You don't have to live with old mindsets, past limitations, or worldly thinking. You have been given the mind of Christ. As you renew your mind, you will experience transformation, clarity, and the supernatural life God has designed for you.

Will you choose to think like a son today?

Discussion Questions

1 . Proverbs 23:7 says, *"As a man thinks in his heart, so is he."* In what ways have your thoughts shaped your current reality —for better or worse? Can you identify a specific area of your life where a shift in thinking could change your outcome?

2 . The chapter shows how Satan's first attack in the Garden was not physical, but mental—through deception. What lies or false perspectives have you struggled with, and how can you actively replace them with God's truth?

3 . Israel was freed from slavery, yet their slave mentality kept them from the Promised Land. What "old mindsets" might still be keeping you from walking fully in God's promises, and what steps can you take to begin renewing your mind in that area?

CHAPTER 2

THE WORD OF GOD – THE ULTIMATE TRANSFORMER

THE MIND'S ANCHOR IN TRUTH

E very believer who desires transformation must ask a crucial question: What is shaping my thinking? In a world filled with opinions, ideologies, and cultural pressures, it is easy to drift away from truth. The enemy's greatest weapon is deception, and his primary target is the mind. Jesus said in John 8:44 that Satan is "the father of lies." If the enemy can plant false ideas about God, ourselves, and reality, he can keep us bound, even as believers.

The only way to combat deception is with truth. Truth is not subjective or open to interpretation—it is found in the Word of God. The Word is not just a book of principles or a historical record—it is the very mind of God revealed to us. When we renew our minds with His Word, we begin to think like Him, see as He sees, and operate in Kingdom reality.

In Romans 12:2, Paul makes it clear that transformation is not possible without mind renewal:

"Do not be conformed to this world, but be transformed by the renewing of your mind, that you may prove what is that good and acceptable and perfect will of God." NKJV

This means that true change begins in the mind, and the Word of God is the tool that reshapes it. Without the Word, our thinking will always default to worldly patterns. But when we immerse ourselves in God's truth, we are set free to live as sons and daughters who walk in divine wisdom, clarity, and power.

The Supernatural Power of the Word

The Word of God is more than just information—it is alive and active. Hebrews 4:12 describes its power:

"For the word of God is living and powerful, and sharper than any two-edged sword, piercing even to the division of soul and spirit, and of joints and marrow, and is a discerner of the thoughts and intents of the heart." NKJV

This passage reveals several key truths:

1. The Word is alive – It is not a dead religious text; it carries the very breath of God (2 Timothy 3:16).
2. The Word is powerful – It has the ability to cut through deception, fear, and every mental stronghold.
3. The Word reveals truth – It exposes the thoughts and intentions of our hearts, separating what is fleshly from what is spiritual.

When we engage with the Word, it renews our minds from the inside out. It dismantles the lies we have believed and replaces them with divine reality.

Jesus: The Model of a Mind Rooted in the Word

Jesus Himself demonstrated the power of a renewed mind grounded in Scripture. In Matthew 4, when Satan tempted Him in the wilderness, Jesus did not argue, reason, or defend Himself with His own words. Instead, He said: "It is written…"

With every attack, Jesus countered the enemy's deception with Scripture. He didn't rely on emotions, opinions, or human reasoning—He stood firm on the Word. This is our model for victory. The enemy will always come with lies, but a mind renewed by the Word of God will not be deceived.

The Word as the Key to Unlocking the Mind of Christ

1 Corinthians 2:9-12, 16 tells us:

"Eye has not seen, nor ear heard, nor have entered into the heart of man the things which God has prepared for those who love Him. But God has revealed them to us through His Spirit… Now we have received, not the spirit of the world, but the Spirit who is from God, that we might know the things that have been freely given to us by God… But we have the mind of Christ." NKJV

This passage is powerful because it reveals that:

- God has prepared things for us that can only be understood through revelation.
- The Spirit of God reveals His thoughts to us.
- We already have the mind of Christ, but we must learn to think with it.

How do we access the thoughts of God? Through His Word. The Bible is God's written thoughts, His revealed will, and His eternal truth. A renewed mind is one that learns to think God's thoughts, believe His truth, and reject every mindset that is contrary to His Word.

The Battle Between Two Mindsets

The Bible speaks of two competing mindsets that war against each other:

1. The Carnal Mind (thinking according to the flesh)
2. The Spiritual Mind (thinking according to the Spirit)

Romans 8:5-8 describes this battle:

"For those who live according to the flesh set their minds on the things of the flesh, but those who live according to the Spirit, the things of the Spirit. For to be carnally minded is death, but to be spiritually minded is life and peace. Because the carnal mind is enmity against God; for it is not subject to the law of God, nor indeed can be. So then, those who are in the flesh cannot please God." NKJV

This scripture makes it clear: a carnal mind cannot submit to God or walk in His will. The carnal mind:

- Relies on emotions and human reasoning.
- Focuses on fear, lack, and impossibility.
- Is influenced by culture rather than the Spirit.
- Leads to spiritual death and frustration.

The renewed mind:

- Is rooted in the truth of God's Word.
- Thinks from Heaven's reality rather than the world's limitations.
- Focuses on faith, power, and supernatural possibilities.
- Leads to peace, clarity, and transformation.

If we desire to walk in supernatural breakthrough, divine wisdom, and unshakable faith, we must abandon carnal thinking and immerse our minds in the truth of God's Word.

Practical Steps to Renew the Mind with the Word

1. Read the Word Daily

- Just as our bodies need daily food, our minds need daily spiritual nourishment.
- Set aside time each day to read, meditate, and engage with Scripture.

2. Speak the Word Over Your Life

- What you declare over yourself matters.
- Replace negative self-talk with biblical truth.

3. Memorize and Meditate on Scripture

- The more Scripture you store in your heart, the more it will shape your thinking.
- Meditation is not just reading—it is allowing the Word to reshape how you think.

4. Filter Every Thought Through the Word
   When a thought enters your mind, ask:

- Does this align with Scripture?
- Is this thought rooted in faith or fear?
- Would Jesus think this way?
- If the thought does not align with the truth, reject it and replace it with Scripture.

5. Let the Holy Spirit Teach You

- The Spirit reveals the deep things of God (1 Corinthians 2:10).

- Ask Him to illuminate Scripture and guide you into truth.

A Renewed Mind is a Transformed Life

The Word of God is the key to unlocking a renewed mind. Without it, we will always default to worldly thinking. But when we immerse ourselves in Scripture, we begin to see, think, and operate in Kingdom reality.

God has already given us the mind of Christ, but we must train ourselves to think with it. Transformation is not just about changing external behavior—it is about thinking with the wisdom of Heaven.

The question is: Will you let the Word shape your mind and transform your life?

Discussion Questions

1 . The chapter emphasizes that deception is the enemy's greatest weapon and that only truth can break it. How have you seen the Word of God expose or dismantle lies in your own life?

2 . Jesus resisted temptation in the wilderness by declaring, *"It is written."* What does this teach us about the importance of knowing Scripture, and how can we apply this in our daily battles of the mind?

3 . Romans 12:2 says transformation happens through renewing the mind. In practical terms, how can you anchor your thoughts in God's Word this week so that your mindset is shaped by Heaven's reality instead of the world's?

CHAPTER 3
KINGDOM THINKING VS. CARNAL THINKING
THE WAR OF TWO MINDSETS

E very believer must come to a realization: There is a war for your mind. The mind is the battlefield where two opposing systems of thought wage war:

1. Kingdom Thinking – The mind renewed by the truth of God's Word and led by the Spirit.
2. Carnal Thinking – The mindset influenced by worldly wisdom, human reasoning, and the flesh.

Paul makes this distinction clear in Romans 8:5-7:

"For those who live according to the flesh set their minds on the things of the flesh, but those who live according to the Spirit, the things of the Spirit. For to be carnally minded is death, but to be spiritually minded is life and peace. Because the carnal mind is enmity against God; for it is not subject to the law of God, nor indeed can be." NKJV

A carnal mind leads to death—spiritually, emotionally, and even physically. It produces fear, confusion, and instability. But a renewed mind leads to life and peace because it is in agreement with God's truth. The renewed mind does not operate based on natural circumstances—it operates based on Kingdom reality. It does not react to problems; it aligns with God's solutions.

In this chapter, we will explore how to recognize, dismantle, and replace carnal thinking with Kingdom thinking so that we can walk in the fullness of God's will and demonstrate His power on the Earth.

The Mindset of the World vs. the Mindset of the Kingdom

The Bible warns us not to be conformed to this world but to be transformed by the renewing of our minds (Romans 12:2). But what does worldly thinking look like, and how does it differ from Kingdom thinking?

Worldly Thinking	Kingdom Thinking
Sees lack	Sees abundance
Reacts in fear	Acts in faith
Lives by sight	Lives by revelation
Focuses on self-preservation	Focuses on God's purpose
Looks for temporary solutions	Operates from eternal perspective
Expects failure & disappointment	Expects God's goodness
Operates in natural wisdom	Functions in supernatural wisdom
Thinks with a victim mentality	Thinks with a sonship mentality

A Kingdom mindset is not optimism without substance—it is rooted in the eternal truth of God's Word. It is not wishful thinking—it is living from the reality of Heaven.

The Danger of Carnal Thinking

The carnal mind is dangerous because it cannot perceive or receive the things of God. Paul explains this in 1 Corinthians 2:14:

"But the natural man does not receive the things of the Spirit of God,

for they are foolishness to him; nor can he know them, because they are spiritually discerned." NKJV

This is why many believers struggle to walk in faith—their minds are still conformed to natural reasoning. They believe in God's power in theory but live as if they are still bound by earthly limitations.

Carnal thinking...

- Causes us to live in fear instead of faith.
- Keeps us focused on problems instead of promises.
- Prevents us from seeing God's provision, protection, and power.

The Israelites are a prime example. God delivered them from Egypt, yet they still thought like slaves. Even after seeing miracles, signs, and wonders, they constantly reverted to doubt and fear.

When they reached the Promised Land, they sent spies to assess the land. The majority returned with a carnal mindset:

"We are like grasshoppers in our own sight, and so we were in their sight." (Numbers 13:33) NKJV

Their wrong thinking robbed them of their inheritance. But Joshua and Caleb—who had a Kingdom mindset—saw the same land and declared:

"If the Lord delights in us, then He will bring us into this land and give it to us." (Numbers 14:8) NKJV

While the rest of Israel saw obstacles, Joshua and Caleb saw opportunity. Your thinking determines your destiny. If you think in alignment with God's promises, you will walk in them. If you think in alignment with fear and limitation, you will stay in the wilderness.

Shifting from Carnal to Kingdom Thinking

Paul makes a powerful statement in 1 Corinthians 2:16:

"For 'who has known the mind of the Lord that he may instruct Him?'
But we have the mind of Christ." NKJV

We already have access to the mind of Christ—but we must learn to think with it. Here's how:

1. Take Every Thought Captive

2 Corinthians 10:5 tells us to: "Cast down arguments and every high thing that exalts itself against the knowledge of God, bringing every thought into captivity to the obedience of Christ." This means:

- Not every thought should be accepted.
- We must filter our thinking through God's truth.
- Every thought that contradicts God's Word must be rejected.

2. Set Your Mind on Things Above

Colossians 3:2 commands: *"Set your mind on things above, not on things on the earth." NKJV*

A renewed mind is one that chooses to focus on the reality of Heaven rather than the chaos of the world.

3. Speak the Language of the Kingdom

Jesus said in Matthew 12:34, *"Out of the abundance of the heart the mouth speaks."* NKJV

Your words reveal what you believe. If your mind is renewed, your speech will reflect it.

Start speaking in agreement with the Kingdom:

- "I am more than a conqueror." (Romans 8:37)
- "God supplies all my needs." (Philippians 4:19)
- "I have the peace of God." (John 14:27)

4. Align Your Actions with Kingdom Thinking

James 2:26 says, "Faith without works is dead." It's not enough to think Kingdom thoughts—we must live them out.

- If you believe God is your provider, live generously.
- If you believe God is your healer, pray for healing with boldness.
- If you believe you have authority, walk in confidence.

Walking in Agreement with God

Amos 3:3 poses a critical question:

"Can two walk together unless they are agreed?" NKJV

Many believers live below their inheritance because they are trying to get God to agree with them instead of aligning with Him. But God will not change His mind to walk with us—we must renew our minds to walk with Him.

A renewed mind is a mind in agreement with:

- God's thoughts
- God's perspective
- God's truth

When we think like sons, we will live like sons. When we align our thoughts with Kingdom reality, we will walk in Kingdom authority.

The Renewed Mind Leads to Transformation

The mind is either the biggest obstacle to our destiny or the greatest key to unlocking it. The enemy wants us to stay conformed to worldly thinking, fear, and limitation. But God calls us to think with the mind of Christ and live in supernatural victory.

Which mindset will you choose?

Will you think according to the flesh, or will you renew your mind and think as a son of God?

The choice is yours, and the journey to Kingdom transformation begins in the mind.

Discussion Questions

1 . What differences do you see between carnal thinking and Kingdom thinking in your own life?

2 . How does fear-based thinking prevent us from walking in faith, and what promises of God can break that cycle?

3 . Joshua and Caleb saw the Promised Land with faith, while others saw giants. What's one area where you need to shift your perspective to see with Kingdom vision?

CHAPTER 4
ALIGNING WITH THE MIND OF CHRIST

THINKING LIKE JESUS

One of the greatest truths in Scripture is found in 1 Corinthians 2:16:

"For 'who has known the mind of the Lord that he may instruct Him?'
But we have the mind of Christ." NKJV

This statement is revolutionary. It does not say that we will one day receive the mind of Christ—it says we already have it. But if this is true, why do so many believers still think in ways that contradict God's truth? Why do fear, doubt, and unbelief often dominate our thoughts?

The reality is that while we possess the mind of Christ, we must learn to think with it. It is like being given the keys to a powerful vehicle—if we don't know how to use it, we will never drive in the authority it provides.

Jesus came not only to reveal the Father but to show us what it means to think and live as sons. He demonstrated a mindset that was fully aligned with the Kingdom, fully submitted to the Father, and fully victorious over sin, sickness, and the power of darkness.

In this chapter, we will examine what it means to align our thinking with the mind of Christ and walk in the same supernatural wisdom, authority, and faith that He did.

What Does It Mean to Have the Mind of Christ?

To have the mind of Christ means that we…

1. See reality from Heaven's perspective.

- Jesus never viewed situations through the lens of lack, fear, or impossibility.
- He always operated from a place of faith and supernatural provision.

2. Think in agreement with the Father.

- In John 5:19, Jesus said, "The Son can do nothing of Himself, but what He sees the Father do."
- He only spoke what the Father spoke and only did what the Father did.

3. Operate in supernatural wisdom.

- Jesus confounded religious leaders with His wisdom because He thought from divine revelation, not human intellect.
- Luke 2:52 says, "Jesus increased in wisdom and stature, and in favor with God and men."

4. Live free from fear and anxiety.

- Jesus never worried about provision, danger, or

opposition because His mind was anchored in the Father's faithfulness.

5. See people through the eyes of love and redemption.

- Where others saw sinners and outcasts, Jesus saw sons and daughters in need of restoration.

If we are to walk in the fullness of our calling, we must learn to think like Jesus.

Jesus' Mindset: The Key to Walking in Supernatural Power

Jesus did not just perform miracles—He carried a mindset that made the miraculous natural. He walked in full authority because His thinking was fully aligned with the Kingdom.

Examples of Jesus' Kingdom Mindset:

1. When faced with lack, He saw abundance.

- In John 6:5-13, Jesus fed over 5,000 people with five loaves and two fish.
- The disciples saw the problem (not enough food), but Jesus saw the solution (supernatural multiplication).

2. When faced with storms, He walked in peace.

- In Mark 4:35-41, a violent storm arose while Jesus and the disciples were in a boat.
- The disciples panicked, but Jesus slept.
- Instead of reacting in fear, Jesus rebuked the storm and restored peace.
- A renewed mind remains at peace even in the midst of chaos.

3. When faced with sickness, He declared healing.

- Jesus never saw sickness as permanent—He always treated it as something subject to the authority of Heaven.
- He commanded healing, knowing that God's will is always to restore.

4. When faced with the cross, He saw victory.

- In Matthew 26:39, Jesus prayed, "Not My will, but Yours be done."
- He did not see the cross as defeat but as the pathway to resurrection power.

This is the mind of Christ—one that sees every circumstance through the lens of Heaven rather than the limitations of Earth.

Shifting Our Thinking to Align with Christ

If we already have the mind of Christ, why do we often default to old ways of thinking? The answer lies in Romans 12:2:

"Do not be conformed to this world, but be transformed by the renewing of your mind, that you may prove what is that good and acceptable and perfect will of God." NKJV

Even though we have access to the mind of Christ, we must intentionally renew our thinking to align with His.
Here's how:

1. Replace Natural Reasoning with Kingdom Revelation

- Stop thinking according to what is natural and start thinking according to what is supernatural.

- Instead of saying, "I don't have enough," declare, "My God shall supply all my needs" (Philippians 4:19).

2. Meditate on the Word of God

- The more we immerse our minds in the Word, the more our thinking aligns with Christ.
- Joshua 1:8 says, "This Book of the Law shall not depart from your mouth, but you shall meditate in it day and night."

3. Take Every Thought Captive

- 2 Corinthians 10:5 commands us to "bring every thought into captivity to the obedience of Christ."
- When a thought contradicts God's Word, we must reject it and replace it with truth.

4. Live by Faith, Not by Sight

- The mind of Christ does not rely on circumstances but on God's promises.
- 2 Corinthians 5:7 says, "For we walk by faith, not by sight."

5. Ask the Holy Spirit for Revelation

- The Holy Spirit is the one who reveals the deep things of God (1 Corinthians 2:10).
- We must daily invite Him to reshape our thinking so that we align with the Kingdom.

Agreement with God: The Key to a Renewed Mind

Amos 3:3 asks, *"Can two walk together unless they are agreed?"*
NKJV

God will not change His mind to walk with us—we must align our thinking with Him.

When we agree with God's thoughts, we begin to:

- See possibilities instead of obstacles.
- Live in peace instead of anxiety.
- Operate in supernatural faith instead of fear.
- Demonstrate God's power instead of living in weakness.

The renewed mind is not just about positive thinking—it is about supernatural agreement with Heaven.

The Invitation to Think Like Jesus

Jesus did not come only to reveal the Father—He came to show us how to think, live, and operate as sons of God. We already have the mind of Christ, but we must align with it, renew our thinking, and reject every thought that contradicts God's truth.

Are you ready to think like Jesus?

- Will you see problems as opportunities for supernatural breakthrough?
- Will you replace fear with faith and anxiety with peace?
- Will you walk in agreement with God's Word rather than the opinions of the world?

The journey to living as a son of God begins with a renewed

mind. The more we align with the mind of Christ, the more we will walk in His power, wisdom, and authority.

Discussion Questions

1 . 1 Corinthians 2:16 says, *"We have the mind of Christ."* What does this mean practically for how you think and live?

2 . Jesus saw storms, sickness, and even the cross through Heaven's perspective. How can you learn to see your challenges the same way?

3 . What daily habits could help you align your thoughts more consistently with the mind of Christ?

CHAPTER 5

BREAKING STRONGHOLDS AND MENTAL BARRIERS
THE POWER OF MINDSETS

E very thought we embrace has the potential to either bring us closer to God's truth or keep us trapped in deception. Our lives are shaped by the dominant patterns of thinking we hold onto, which is why the Bible repeatedly emphasizes the importance of renewing the mind.

The greatest battles we face are not against external circumstances but against the strongholds in our own minds. These strongholds are not physical walls but mental fortresses built by wrong beliefs, fears, and past experiences.

2 Corinthians 10:3-5 describes this battle:

"For though we walk in the flesh, we do not war according to the flesh. For the weapons of our warfare are not carnal but mighty in God for pulling down strongholds, casting down arguments and every high thing that exalts itself against the knowledge of God, bringing every thought into captivity to the obedience of Christ." NKJV

This passage reveals that:

- Strongholds are wrong ways of thinking that exalt themselves against God's truth.

- We must actively tear down these deceptive mindsets.
- Every thought that contradicts God's Word must be taken captive and brought into alignment with Christ.

In this chapter, we will identify common mental strongholds, expose how they operate, and learn how to demolish them with the truth of God's Word.

What is a Stronghold?

A stronghold is a deeply entrenched thought pattern, belief system, or mindset that resists the truth of God's Word. Strongholds shape the way we see God, ourselves, and the world.

A stronghold can be:

- A lie that we have believed for so long that it feels like truth.
- A cycle of fear, doubt, or insecurity that keeps us bound.
- A negative expectation that prevents us from receiving God's best.

The Greek word for stronghold (ochuroma) refers to a fortified prison. This means that strongholds trap us, keeping us from walking in freedom and transformation.

Common Mental Strongholds

Let's examine some of the most common strongholds that hinder believers from stepping into a renewed mind and a victorious life.

1. The Orphan Mindset

Stronghold: "I am alone. God doesn't really care about me." An orphan mindset causes people to:

- Live in fear of rejection instead of resting in sonship.
- Feel unworthy of God's love and blessings.
- Strive for approval instead of resting in God's grace.

Truth to Break It:

- Romans 8:15 – "You did not receive the spirit of bondage again to fear, but you received the Spirit of adoption by whom we cry out, 'Abba, Father.'"
- Galatians 4:7 – "You are no longer a slave but a son, and if a son, then an heir of God through Christ."

2. The Victim Mentality

Stronghold: "I can't change. My past defines me." A victim mindset makes people believe:

- They are powerless to change.
- Their circumstances control their destiny.
- Their past dictates their future.

Truth to Break It:

- 2 Corinthians 5:17 – "If anyone is in Christ, he is a new creation; old things have passed away; behold, all things have become new."
- Philippians 4:13 – "I can do all things through Christ who strengthens me."

3. The Poverty Mindset

Stronghold: "There's never enough. I will always struggle." A poverty mindset leads to:

- Fear of giving and generosity.
- Constant worry about provision.
- Doubting God's ability to provide supernaturally.

Truth to Break It:

- Philippians 4:19 – "My God shall supply all your need according to His riches in glory by Christ Jesus."
- Matthew 6:33 – "Seek first the kingdom of God and His righteousness, and all these things shall be added to you."

4. The Religious Spirit

Stronghold: "God only loves me when I perform well." A religious mindset:

- Bases identity on works instead of grace.
- Creates spiritual pride or self-condemnation.
- Focuses on rules and rituals rather than relationship.

Truth to Break It:

- Ephesians 2:8-9 – "By grace you have been saved through faith, and that not of yourselves; it is the gift of God, not of works, lest anyone should boast."
- Romans 8:1 – "There is therefore now no condemnation to those who are in Christ Jesus."

5. The Fear of Man

Stronghold: "What people think about me is more important than what God says." This stronghold leads to:

- Fear of rejection and people-pleasing.
- Compromising truth to gain approval.
- A constant need for validation.

Truth to Break It:

- Galatians 1:10 – "If I still pleased men, I would not be a bondservant of Christ."
- Proverbs 29:25 – "The fear of man brings a snare, but whoever trusts in the Lord shall be safe."

How to Demolish Strongholds
1. Identify the Lies

- Ask yourself: What thought patterns are keeping me from walking in freedom?
- The Holy Spirit will reveal wrong beliefs that need to be broken.

2. Replace Lies with Truth

- Every stronghold is built on a lie, and every lie must be replaced with God's Word.
- Find scriptures that directly contradict the lie and declare them over your life.

3. Renew Your Mind Daily

- Romans 12:2 tells us that transformation comes through renewing the mind.
- This is not a one-time event but a daily process.

4. Take Thoughts Captive

- 2 Corinthians 10:5 says to bring every thought into obedience to Christ.
- When a negative or fearful thought arises, reject it and declare the truth instead.

5. Align Your Thinking with the Mind of Christ

- Jesus never thought from a place of fear, insecurity, or lack.
- We must train our minds to think as He thinks.

Walking in Freedom and Authority

Once strongholds are broken, we must actively walk in the truth.

1. Declare Who You Are in Christ

- Speak your identity daily until your mind fully embraces it.
- Example: "I am a son/daughter of God. I have authority. I live in abundance and peace."

2. Stay in the Word

- Joshua 1:8 – "This Book of the Law shall not depart from your mouth, but you shall meditate in it day and night."
- The Word of God is the foundation of a renewed mind.

3. Live Boldly in Your New Mindset

- If you have broken the fear of man, start stepping out in faith.

- If you have broken the poverty mindset, start living with generosity.
- If you have broken the orphan mindset, start walking in confidence as a son/daughter.

The Renewed Mind is a Free Mind

A renewed mind is a liberated mind. It is a mind that rejects deception, aligns with truth, and walks in Kingdom authority.

- What strongholds are holding you back?
- What lies have you believed that need to be broken?
- Are you willing to allow the Holy Spirit to transform your thinking?

The journey to transformation begins when we tear down mental barriers and embrace the mind of Christ. The choice is ours:

Will we continue to live in limitation, or will we step into the fullness of Kingdom thinking?

Discussion Questions

1 . What stronghold (fear, orphan mindset, victim mentality, etc.) do you most relate to, and why?

2 . 2 Corinthians 10:5 says we must "take every thought captive." How can you put this into practice when negative or fearful thoughts arise?

3 . What truth from Scripture do you need to declare over your life to break a lingering mental barrier?

CHAPTER 6

THE SUPERNATURAL POWER OF A RENEWED MIND

THINKING FROM HEAVEN'S PERSPECTIVE

A renewed mind is more than just thinking differently—it is living differently. It is the gateway to supernatural transformation, divine wisdom, and Kingdom authority. Paul makes this clear in Romans 12:2:

"Do not be conformed to this world, but be transformed by the renewing of your mind, that you may prove what is that good and acceptable and perfect will of God." NKJV

Transformation begins when we stop thinking like the world and start thinking like God. A renewed mind does not react to circumstances; it shapes them. It does not accept problems as permanent; it sees them as opportunities for supernatural intervention.

Jesus lived with a fully renewed mind—one that was in constant agreement with Heaven. As a result, He operated in supernatural wisdom, faith, and authority. This same reality is available to us. In this chapter, we will explore how a renewed mind unlocks the supernatural, increases faith, and brings Heaven's reality to Earth.

A Renewed Mind Sees the Unseen

The natural mind is limited by what it can see, hear, and understand. It relies on logic, past experiences, and human reasoning. But a renewed mind operates from faith, not sight.

2 Corinthians 5:7 declares: *"For we walk by faith, not by sight."* NKJV

This means:

- We do not base our decisions on what we see but on what God has spoken.
- We do not respond to fear and doubt but to faith and revelation.
- We do not limit our thinking to earthly possibilities but expect Heaven's solutions.

Jesus demonstrated this kind of supernatural thinking.

Example: The Raising of Lazarus (John 11)

- When Jesus heard that Lazarus was sick, He did not panic or rush to heal him. Instead, He said, "This sickness is not unto death, but for the glory of God." (John 11:4)
- Even after Lazarus died, Jesus did not see death as final. He declared, "I am the resurrection and the life." (John 11:25)
- Where others saw a hopeless situation, Jesus saw an opportunity for God's glory.
- A renewed mind does not accept natural limitations— it sees God's power beyond them.

The Mind of Christ Thinks with Supernatural Authority

We are not meant to live as victims of circumstances—we are called to shape the world around us with Kingdom authority. Jesus did not just react to situations—He took dominion over them.

Example: Jesus Calming the Storm (Mark 4:35-41)

- While crossing the sea, a violent storm arose, threatening to sink the boat.
- The disciples panicked, thinking they were about to die.
- But Jesus was sleeping, completely unshaken by the storm.
- When the disciples woke Him, He did not panic—He spoke with authority: "Peace, be still!" (Mark 4:39)
- The wind and waves immediately obeyed.

A renewed mind thinks like Jesus:

- It does not fear the storm; it commands the storm to be still.
- It does not see obstacles; it sees opportunities for God's power.
- It does not wait for circumstances to change; it brings Heaven's authority into the situation.

A Renewed Mind Brings Heaven to Earth

Jesus taught His disciples to pray a radical prayer:

"Your kingdom come, Your will be done on earth as it is in heaven."
(Matthew 6:10) NKJV

This prayer reveals that:

- Heaven is the standard for how we should think and live.
- God's will is for His supernatural reality to invade Earth.
- A renewed mind does not wait for Heaven—it brings Heaven into the present.

This means:

- Sickness must bow because in Heaven, there is no sickness.
- Lack must be replaced with provision because Heaven has unlimited resources.
- Fear and depression must be broken because Heaven is filled with peace and joy.

A renewed mind does not live in reaction to the world—it brings the reality of Heaven into every situation.

The Connection Between a Renewed Mind and Faith

One of the greatest results of renewing the mind is increased faith. Romans 10:17 tells us:

"Faith comes by hearing, and hearing by the word of God." NKJV

This means that:

- Faith is not something we try to produce—it is the natural result of a renewed mind.
- The more we fill our minds with God's truth, the easier it becomes to believe.
- A mind aligned with God's Word naturally expects miracles, provision, and breakthrough.

Example: The Woman with the Issue of Blood (Mark 5:25-34)

- This woman had been sick for twelve years with a condition that doctors could not heal.
- But she heard about Jesus and began to renew her thinking.
- She declared, "If I can just touch His garment, I will be healed."
- Her renewed mind produced faith, and when she touched Jesus, she was instantly healed.

A renewed mind:

- Stops doubting God's power.
- Thinks with bold faith instead of fear.
- Sees impossibilities as opportunities for God to move.

How to Cultivate a Supernaturally Renewed Mind

1. Fill Your Mind with God's Word

- Joshua 1:8 – "This Book of the Law shall not depart from your mouth, but you shall meditate in it day and night."
- The more Scripture saturates your mind, the more it will align with God's thoughts.

2. Refuse to Accept Earthly Limitations

- Mark 9:23 – "If you can believe, all things are possible to him who believes."
- Never let past disappointments define what you believe about God.

3. Take Every Thought Captive

- 2 Corinthians 10:5 – "Bring every thought into captivity to the obedience of Christ."
- Reject any thought that contradicts what God says.

4. Declare What You Believe

- Proverbs 18:21 – "Death and life are in the power of the tongue."
- Speak Kingdom truth over yourself and your circumstances daily.

5. Partner with the Holy Spirit

- 1 Corinthians 2:10 – "The Spirit searches all things, yes, the deep things of God."
- Ask the Holy Spirit to show you how to think from Heaven's perspective.

Walking in Supernatural Thinking

The supernatural is not reserved for a select few—it is the natural result of a renewed mind. A carnal mind lives in fear, lack, and doubt. A renewed mind walks in faith, abundance, and supernatural power. Jesus lived with a completely renewed mind, and as a result:

- He saw solutions before problems arose.
- He spoke to storms, healed the sick, and raised the dead.
- He never questioned the Father's will but carried it out with full confidence.

This same mindset is available to us.

The question is:

- Will you think like Heaven or remain bound by earthly limitations?
- Will you allow God's Word to shape your thinking until faith becomes your natural response?
- Will you step into the supernatural lifestyle that a renewed mind unlocks?

Your transformation begins when you choose to align your thoughts with the mind of Christ.

Are you ready?

Discussion Questions

1 . A renewed mind doesn't just see problems—it sees opportunities for God's power. Where in your life do you need to shift from natural reasoning to supernatural faith?

2 . Jesus calmed the storm by speaking with authority. How can you use Kingdom authority in your own circumstances?

3 . What practical step can you take this week to live more fully from Heaven's perspective instead of earthly limitations?

CHAPTER 7
LIVING FROM THE REALITY OF HEAVEN
SEEING THE WORLD THROUGH HEAVEN'S EYES

One of the most transformative aspects of a renewed mind is learning to live from the reality of Heaven rather than reacting to the reality of the world. When Jesus taught His disciples to pray, He gave them a radical request:

"Your kingdom come, Your will be done on earth as it is in heaven."
(Matthew 6:10) NKJV

This statement reveals a foundational truth:

- Heaven is not just a place we go when we die—it is the blueprint for how we should live now.
- A renewed mind is one that sees, thinks, and operates from Heaven's perspective.
- If it is not permitted in Heaven, it should not be accepted on Earth.

This means that sickness, fear, poverty, oppression, and despair are illegal in the life of a believer. A renewed mind does not just accept problems as normal—it expects Heaven's solutions to manifest in every situation.

In this chapter, we will explore how to shift our mindset from an earthly perspective to a Kingdom perspective, learning to think, live, and act from the reality of Heaven.

Jesus Lived from Heaven's Reality

Jesus never operated from an earthly perspective. He saw everything from the viewpoint of the Father's Kingdom. This is why He was able to:

- Calm storms instead of fearing them.
- Multiply food instead of worrying about lack.
- Heal sickness instead of accepting it as normal.
- See sinners as sons and daughters instead of rejecting them.

Jesus functioned in this mindset because He saw what the Father was doing and aligned with it.

"The Son can do nothing of Himself, but what He sees the Father do; for whatever He does, the Son also does in like manner." (John 5:19) NKJV

His actions were not reactions to the world—they were responses to Heaven. A renewed mind does not react to problems—it responds with Kingdom authority.

The Difference Between an Earthly Mindset and a Kingdom Mindset

A renewed mind is one that sees everything through the lens of Heaven.

Earthly Mindset	Kingdom Mindset
Sees lack	Sees abundance
Sees problems	Sees solutions
Lives in fear	Lives by faith
Focuses on circumstances	Focuses on God's promises
Accepts sickness as normal	Believes healing is God's will
Lives for survival	Lives for Kingdom purpose

A renewed mind does not conform to the world's way of thinking—it is transformed by God's truth.

"Do not be conformed to this world, but be transformed by the renewing of your mind." (Romans 12:2) NKJV

A Renewed Mind Expects Heaven's Reality to Manifest

A believer who thinks from the reality of Heaven begins to expect:

- Healing instead of sickness
- Provision instead of lack
- Victory instead of defeat
- Favor instead of struggle
- Supernatural solutions instead of hopelessness

This is not denial of reality—it is aligning with a higher reality. Paul confirms this in Colossians 3:2:

"Set your mind on things above, not on things on the earth." NKJV

A renewed mind does not ignore the natural world—it chooses to live from a supernatural one.

Examples of Kingdom Thinking in Action

1. Jesus Feeding the 5,000 (John 6:1-14)

- The disciples saw lack and said, "We don't have enough."
- Jesus saw abundance and took what they had, blessed it, and multiplied it.
- A renewed mind does not focus on what is missing—it partners with Heaven to bring increase.

2. Jesus and Jairus' Daughter (Mark 5:35-42)

- The people saw death and hopelessness.
- Jesus said, "The child is not dead but sleeping."
- Where others saw an end, Jesus saw an opportunity for resurrection.
- A renewed mind does not accept finality when God's power can bring life.

3. Peter Walking on Water (Matthew 14:22-33)

- When Peter looked at the storm, he began to sink.
- When he fixed his eyes on Jesus, he walked in the supernatural.
- A renewed mind does not focus on the storm—it focuses on the One who has authority over it.

These stories show that miracles happen when we shift from earthly thinking to Kingdom thinking.

How to Live from the Reality of Heaven

1. See Situations Through Heaven's Perspective

- Ask: "How does God see this situation?"
- Shift your focus from problems to promises.

2. Speak the Language of the Kingdom

- Your words should reflect faith, not fear.
- Speak what God says, not what circumstances say.
- Proverbs 18:21 – "Death and life are in the power of the tongue."

3. Align Your Thinking with God's Word

- If your thoughts contradict Scripture, replace them.
- 2 Corinthians 10:5 – "Take every thought captive to the obedience of Christ."

4. Expect Supernatural Solutions

- A renewed mind believes that God has already provided the answer.
- Philippians 4:19 – "My God shall supply all your needs according to His riches in glory."

5. Partner with the Holy Spirit

- The Holy Spirit reveals what is available in Heaven so we can manifest it on Earth.
- 1 Corinthians 2:9-10 – "God has revealed them to us through His Spirit."

Agreement with God Brings Supernatural Results

Amos 3:3 asks: *"Can two walk together unless they are agreed?"*
NKJV

God will not change His mind to align with our thinking—we must change our thinking to align with Him. A renewed mind walks in agreement with Heaven. When we think like God, we begin to:

- See opportunities instead of obstacles.
- Live with bold faith instead of fear.
- Operate in supernatural provision instead of lack.

A renewed mind is a mind that walks in unity with Heaven's reality.

Living as a Citizen of Heaven

Philippians 3:20 reminds us: *"Our citizenship is in heaven."* NKJV

We are not just waiting to go to Heaven—we are called to bring Heaven to Earth. The renewed mind does not ask, "What is possible on Earth?"—it asks, "What is available in Heaven?"

The question is:

- Will you continue to live limited by earthly thinking?
- Or will you renew your mind and step into the reality of Heaven?

You were created to think, live, and operate from a supernatural realm. The choice is yours—will you align your mind with the reality of Heaven today?

Discussion Questions

1 . Jesus taught us to pray, *"Your Kingdom come, Your will be done on earth as it is in Heaven."* What does it look like to live from Heaven's reality in daily life?

2 . What earthly mindset (fear, lack, doubt) do you need to replace with Heaven's reality (faith, abundance, peace)?

3 . Which example from Scripture (feeding the 5,000, Jairus' daughter, Peter walking on water) most inspires you to think from Heaven's perspective—and why?

CHAPTER 8
TRANSFORMING CULTURE THROUGH RENEWED THINKING
THE RENEWED MIND AS A CATALYST FOR CHANGE

The transformation of the world begins with the transformation of the mind. Many believers desire to see revival, societal change, and cultural reformation, but few recognize that it starts with how we think. Proverbs 23:7 declares:

"As a man thinks in his heart, so is he." NKJV

If we desire to shift culture, we must first shift our mindset. A renewed mind does not conform to the thinking of the world but transforms it by introducing Kingdom realities.

Romans 12:2 gives us the blueprint:

"Do not be conformed to this world, but be transformed by the renewing of your mind, that you may prove what is that good and acceptable and perfect will of God." NKJV

A renewed mind is not just for personal growth—it is meant to influence families, communities, and nations. In this chapter, we will explore how Kingdom-minded believers are called to bring Heaven's influence into government, business, education, media, and every sphere of culture.

Jesus' Model for Cultural Transformation

Jesus did not come just to save individuals—He came to bring the Kingdom of God into every sphere of life.

In Luke 4:18-19, Jesus declared His mission:

"The Spirit of the Lord is upon Me, because He has anointed Me to preach the gospel to the poor; He has sent Me to heal the brokenhearted, to proclaim liberty to the captives and recovery of sight to the blind, to set at liberty those who are oppressed; to proclaim the acceptable year of the Lord." NKJV

Jesus' Kingdom mission included:

- Preaching truth that liberates minds.
- Healing hearts so people can live in freedom.
- Breaking oppression so entire communities could be restored.

Wherever Jesus went, He challenged the mindsets that kept people in bondage. He confronted religious systems, governmental corruption, and societal oppression with Kingdom truth. His goal was not just personal salvation but the transformation of culture.

How a Renewed Mind Impacts Society

A believer with a renewed mind does not withdraw from the world—they bring transformation to it. Jesus said:

"You are the light of the world. A city that is set on a hill cannot be hidden." (Matthew 5:14) NKJV

Light shifts atmospheres. It does not adapt to darkness—it overcomes it. A renewed mind influences culture by:

1. Challenging Cultural Lies with Kingdom Truth

- The world says, "Truth is subjective."
- The Kingdom says, "God's Word is the absolute truth." (John 17:17)
- A believer with a renewed mind boldly declares the truth in a world of deception.

2. Bringing Heaven's Solutions into Society

- Joseph's renewed mind brought economic solutions to Egypt during famine. (Genesis 41)
- Daniel's renewed mind shifted government policies in Babylon. (Daniel 6)
- Esther's renewed mind delivered an entire nation from destruction. (Esther 4)
- A believer with a renewed mind sees problems as opportunities for divine strategy.

3. Living with Unshakable Integrity in Corrupt Systems

- The world says, "Compromise is necessary for success."
- The Kingdom says, "Righteousness exalts a nation." (Proverbs 14:34)
- A believer with a renewed mind walks in integrity, even when surrounded by corruption.

4. Demonstrating the Supernatural in Everyday Life

- The world says, "Miracles are not for today."
- The Kingdom says, "These signs will follow those who believe." (Mark 16:17)

- A believer with a renewed mind operates in supernatural power, bringing Heaven's reality into workplaces, schools, and governments.

Transforming the Seven Mountains of Culture

A renewed mind is not meant to stay inside the four walls of the church—it is meant to influence every sphere of culture. The Seven Mountains of Influence represent the key areas of society that shape the way people think:

1. Government – Bringing righteous leadership and Kingdom justice.
2. Education – Teaching truth and shaping future generations.
3. Business – Establishing godly ethics and supernatural provision.
4. Media – Restoring truth in storytelling and reporting.
5. Arts & Entertainment – Creating films, music, and art that reflect God's beauty and truth.
6. Family – Strengthening biblical values in homes.
7. Religion – Equipping the church to walk in Kingdom authority.

A renewed mind understands that believers are called to influence these mountains with Kingdom wisdom, truth, and power.

"The kingdoms of this world have become the kingdoms of our Lord and of His Christ." (Revelation 11:15) NKJV

The goal of the renewed mind is not escape—it is occupation and transformation.

Keys to Transforming Culture Through Renewed Thinking

1. Engage Culture Without Compromising Truth

- Jesus ate with sinners but never adopted their ways. (Luke 19:10)
- Daniel served in a pagan government but never bowed to false gods. (Daniel 6:10)
- A renewed mind engages the world while remaining rooted in Kingdom values.

2. Think Like a Son, Not a Servant

- Servants wait for permission—sons take dominion.
- A renewed mind does not think, "What is allowed?" but "What has God called me to do?"

3. Speak with Kingdom Boldness

- Paul did not hide his faith in front of kings—he boldly declared Christ. (Acts 26:27-29)
- A renewed mind is not afraid to proclaim truth in the face of opposition.

4. Bring Solutions, Not Just Criticism

- The world does not need more complaints—it needs Kingdom answers.
- Joseph did not just interpret Pharaoh's dream—he offered economic solutions. (Genesis 41:33-36)

5. Walk in Supernatural Favor and Wisdom

- Proverbs 3:5-6 – "Trust in the Lord with all your heart... and He will direct your paths."
- When your mind is renewed, favor and wisdom follow you in every area of life.

Agreement with God Brings Cultural Transformation

Amos 3:3 asks: *"Can two walk together unless they are agreed?"*
NKJV

Cultural change begins when believers agree with Heaven and reject the lies of the world.

A renewed mind is dangerous to the enemy because:

- It sees what is possible through faith.
- It believes that revival can touch every nation.
- It declares truth in a world filled with deception.

We are not just called to survive in culture—we are called to shape it with Kingdom truth.

The Renewed Mind is a Cultural Weapon

The battle for society is ultimately a battle for the mind.

- Whoever controls the way people think controls the future of nations.
- A renewed mind does not adapt to culture—it transforms it.

The question is:

- Will you continue to conform to the world's way of thinking?
- Or will you renew your mind and become a Kingdom influencer in every sphere of society?

The world is waiting for believers who will think with the

mind of Christ, walk in bold faith, and bring Heaven's culture into every area of life.

Are you ready to be one of them?

Discussion Questions

1 . How can renewing your mind affect not just your life but your family, community, or workplace?

2 . The chapter talks about the Seven Mountains of influence. Which area (family, business, government, etc.) do you feel called to impact with Kingdom thinking?

3 . What cultural lies do you see in society today that need to be confronted with Kingdom truth?

CHAPTER 9

THE ROLE OF FAITH IN RENEWING THE MIND
FAITH AS THE ENGINE OF A RENEWED MIND

One of the greatest revelations in the Christian life is that faith is not just believing in God—it is thinking like God. Faith is the operating system of Heaven. Everything in the Kingdom functions by faith, and without it, we cannot fully walk in the transformation that a renewed mind brings. Hebrews 11:6 declares:

"But without faith it is impossible to please Him, for he who comes to God must believe that He is, and that He is a rewarder of those who diligently seek Him." NKJV

A renewed mind is one that has been rewired to function in faith instead of fear, expectation instead of doubt, and confidence in God instead of dependence on human logic.

- The natural mind sees problems and impossibilities.
- The renewed mind sees promises and opportunities.
- The natural mind operates by human reasoning.
- The renewed mind operates by faith in God's word.

In this chapter, we will explore how faith is essential to mind renewal and how aligning our thoughts with faith transforms the way we live, pray, and experience God's power.

Faith and the Battle for the Mind

The greatest battle in the life of a believer happens in the mind. Every situation we face presents a choice: Will we think from faith or fear? Will we believe God's promises or react to circumstances? Paul understood this battle, which is why he commanded us in 2 Corinthians 10:5:

"Casting down arguments and every high thing that exalts itself against the knowledge of God, bringing every thought into captivity to the obedience of Christ." NKJV

This means:

- Doubt is an argument against God's truth.
- Fear is a stronghold that must be broken.
- Every thought that contradicts faith must be taken captive.

A renewed mind refuses to let fear shape its perspective. It chooses faith as the foundation of every thought.

Jesus and the Faith Mindset

Jesus never thought from a place of doubt or unbelief. He operated fully from faith because He saw every situation through Heaven's perspective.

Example 1: Jesus Feeding the 5,000 (John 6:5-13)

- The disciples saw lack and said, "We don't have enough."

- Jesus saw abundance and blessed what they had until it multiplied.
- A renewed mind does not focus on what is missing—it operates in faith and sees provision.

Example 2: Jesus Raising Lazarus (John 11:1-44)

- When Jesus heard Lazarus was sick, He did not panic.
- Instead of responding to fear, He said, "This sickness is not unto death, but for the glory of God." (John 11:4)
- Where others saw a dead man, Jesus saw resurrection.
- A renewed mind does not accept natural limitations— it expects supernatural results.

Faith is not denial of reality—it is agreement with a greater reality.

Faith as the Key to Thinking Like God

Isaiah 55:8-9 reveals an important truth about how God thinks:

"For My thoughts are not your thoughts, nor are your ways My ways," says the Lord. "For as the heavens are higher than the earth, so are My ways higher than your ways, and My thoughts than your thoughts." NKJV

If we want to think like God, we must embrace faith as the foundation of our thinking. A renewed mind does not function by what is seen, but by what God has spoken.

How Faith Transforms the Mind

1. Faith Sees What the Natural Mind Cannot Perceive

- The natural mind sees walls—faith sees Jericho falling.
- The natural mind sees giants—faith sees a Promised Land to possess.
- The natural mind sees lack—faith sees Heaven's unlimited resources.

2. Faith Releases Supernatural Wisdom

- James 1:5-6 – "If any of you lacks wisdom, let him ask of God, who gives to all liberally… but let him ask in faith, with no doubting."
- A renewed mind thinks from divine wisdom instead of human understanding.

3. Faith Rewires Our Perspective on Challenges

- Romans 8:28 – "All things work together for good to those who love God."
- A renewed mind sees trials as opportunities for God's power to be revealed.

How to Strengthen Faith for a Renewed Mind

Faith is not a feeling—it is a discipline. If we want to renew our minds to think in faith, we must train ourselves to function in faith daily.

1. Immerse Yourself in God's Word

"Faith comes by hearing, and hearing by the word of God." (Romans 10:17) NKJV

- The more we consume God's truth, the more our minds align with faith.

2. Reject Thoughts of Fear and Doubt

"God has not given us a spirit of fear, but of power, love, and a sound mind." (2 Timothy 1:7) NKJV

When fear arises, replace it with the truth of God's promises.

3. Declare the Truth Over Your Life
"Death and life are in the power of the tongue." (Proverbs 18:21) NKJV

- Speak in agreement with faith, not in agreement with fear.

4. Act in Obedience Even When You Don't Feel It

"Faith without works is dead." (James 2:26) NKJV

- Faith is not just about what we believe—it is about how we act.

5. Surround Yourself with Faith-Filled People

"He who walks with wise men will be wise." (Proverbs 13:20) NKJV

- Stay connected to people who encourage faith, not feed doubt.

Agreement with God Brings a Faith-Filled Mind

Amos 3:3 asks: *"Can two walk together unless they are agreed?"*
NKJV

If we want to walk with God, we must think like Him. That means faith must be our default mindset.

- A mind filled with doubt will always resist God's plans.
- A mind renewed in faith will always step into God's promises.

A faith-filled mind:

- Sees what God is doing before it manifests.
- Declares God's promises before they come to pass.
- Acts boldly even when circumstances look impossible.

A Renewed Mind Lives by Faith

Faith is the lifeblood of a transformed mind. It is the foundation of how we:

- Think.
- Pray.
- Speak.
- Make decisions.

A renewed mind rejects doubt, embraces faith, and expects Heaven's reality to manifest.

The question is:

- Will you continue thinking according to the world's limitations?
- Or will you renew your mind to think and live in the fullness of faith?

You were created to think in faith, live in faith, and operate in supernatural confidence.

Are you ready to align your mind with the faith of Heaven?

Discussion Questions

1 . How does faith reframe the way we see problems, challenges, and opportunities?

2 . In what ways do doubt and fear try to argue against God's truth in your life?

3 . What promise of God do you need to hold onto by faith right now, even when circumstances say otherwise?

CHAPTER 10

WALKING IN VICTORY – A RENEWED MIND AS A LIFESTYLE

VICTORY BEGINS IN THE MIND

Many believers struggle in their Christian walk, not because they lack salvation, but because they lack a renewed mindset that sustains victory.

Proverbs 23:7 declares: *"As a man thinks in his heart, so is he."* NKJV

Victory in life does not come from circumstances—it comes from thinking in alignment with God's truth. The battle for victory is not external—it is internal. A renewed mind is not an event—it is a lifestyle. Paul instructs in Romans 12:2:

"Do not be conformed to this world, but be transformed by the renewing of your mind." NKJV

Transformation is not just a one-time experience with God—it is a daily commitment to think, live, and act according to His Word. In this final chapter, we will explore how to walk in sustained victory through the daily practice of renewing the mind.

Victory Is Sustained by Right Thinking

Many believers experience temporary breakthroughs but return to old struggles because they never change how they think. Jesus explained this principle in Luke 11:24-26, describing how a demon that leaves a person will return if the house is left empty.

"When an unclean spirit goes out of a man, he goes through dry places, seeking rest; and finding none, he says, 'I will return to my house from which I came.' And when he comes, he finds it swept and put in order. Then he goes and takes with him seven other spirits more wicked than himself, and they enter and dwell there; and the last state of that man is worse than the first." NKJV

This passage reveals a critical truth:

- Deliverance alone does not sustain victory.
- Transformation comes through mind renewal.

If we do not fill our minds with God's truth, old strongholds will try to return. A renewed mind ensures that victory is maintained.

What Walking in Victory Looks Like

A victorious believer does not live in reaction to circumstances but lives in dominion over them. Here's what sustained victory looks like:

1. Freedom from Sin's Control

- A renewed mind rejects the lies of temptation and lives in righteousness.
- Romans 6:14 – "For sin shall not have dominion over you, for you are not under law but under grace."

2. A Life of Peace and Joy

- A renewed mind does not entertain fear, stress, or anxiety.
- Philippians 4:7 – "And the peace of God, which surpasses all understanding, will guard your hearts and minds through Christ Jesus."

3. Boldness and Confidence in Identity

- A renewed mind knows that it is a son, not a slave.
- Romans 8:15 – "You did not receive the spirit of bondage again to fear, but you received the Spirit of adoption."

4. Supernatural Faith as the Default Response

- A renewed mind sees impossibilities as opportunities for God's power.
- Mark 9:23 – "If you can believe, all things are possible to him who believes."

5. A Life That Influences Others for the Kingdom

- A renewed mind does not live selfishly—it advances the Kingdom.
- Matthew 5:14 – "You are the light of the world. A city that is set on a hill cannot be hidden."

Sustained victory is not about trying harder—it is about thinking differently.

How to Maintain a Renewed Mind Daily

1. Guard Your Thought Life

- What we allow into our minds determines the direction of our lives.
- Philippians 4:8 – "Whatever things are true, noble, just, pure, lovely, of good report… meditate on these things."
- Practical Step: Cut off negative influences that pollute your thinking.

2. Stay Rooted in the Word of God

- The Word is the food of a renewed mind.
- Joshua 1:8 – "This Book of the Law shall not depart from your mouth, but you shall meditate in it day and night."
- Practical Step: Read, study, and declare Scripture daily.

3. Take Every Thought Captive

- Not every thought should be entertained.
- 2 Corinthians 10:5 – "Bringing every thought into captivity to the obedience of Christ."
- Practical Step: When a negative or fearful thought arises, immediately reject it and replace it with truth.

4. Speak Words of Life and Agreement with God

- Your words shape your reality.
- Proverbs 18:21 – "Death and life are in the power of the tongue."
- Practical Step: Make daily declarations aligned with God's truth.

5. Walk in the Spirit, Not the Flesh

- The Holy Spirit is the source of transformation.
- Romans 8:5 – "For those who live according to the flesh set their minds on the things of the flesh, but those who live according to the Spirit, the things of the Spirit."
- Practical Step: Start each day by yielding to the Holy Spirit in prayer.

6. Surround Yourself with Kingdom-Minded People

- Who you walk with determines who you become.
- Proverbs 13:20 – "He who walks with wise men will be wise."
- Practical Step: Stay connected to people who challenge you to think and live according to the Kingdom.

Sustained victory is not about spiritual highs—it is about consistent, daily renewal.

The Power of Agreement with God

Amos 3:3 asks: *"Can two walk together unless they are agreed?"*
NKJV

A renewed mind walks in agreement with God in every area.

- Agreement with God produces transformation.
- Disagreement with God leads to struggle and delay.

Victory is the result of choosing daily to align our thoughts with Heaven. A renewed mind:

- Refuses to entertain defeat.
- Speaks only in alignment with God's promises.

- Sees every challenge as an opportunity for breakthrough.

Victory is Your New Normal

Walking in victory is not just for a select few—it is the inheritance of every believer. Romans 8:37 declares:

"Yet in all these things we are more than conquerors through Him who loved us." NKJV

Victory is not something we have to strive for—it is something we live from. The question is:

- Will you continue thinking as a victim, or will you walk in the mindset of a victor?
- Will you conform to worldly thinking, or will you commit to daily renewal?
- Will you live a life limited by human reasoning, or will you embrace the supernatural thinking of the Kingdom?

The renewed mind is the key to:

- Overcoming sin
- Walking in supernatural faith
- Bringing Heaven's reality to Earth
- Fulfilling your divine purpose

This is your invitation to step into a lifestyle of victory.

Will you say yes?

Final Charge: The Call to a Renewed Life

As we close this journey, I challenge you to:

1. Refuse to live with a mind conformed to the world.
2. Make renewing your mind a daily discipline.
3. Think, speak, and live from Heaven's perspective.
4. Step into your calling as a son or daughter of God.

The world is waiting for believers who will rise up, think with the mind of Christ, and walk in the power of a transformed life.

Will you be one of them?

Discussion Questions

1 . Victory is sustained through right thinking. What patterns of thought help you stay in daily victory with God?

2 . Why do you think many believers experience breakthrough but then return to old struggles? How can a renewed mind prevent this?

3 . What is one mindset shift you can commit to this week that will help you walk in consistent victory?

CONCLUSION
THE INVITATION TO A TRANSFORMED LIFE

The Journey of Renewal is Just Beginning

You have now reached the end of this book, but in reality, the journey of renewing the mind never ends. Transformation is not a one-time event—it is a daily pursuit. Each day, we are presented with a choice:

- Will we think like the world, or will we think like Heaven?
- Will we conform to culture, or will we be transformed by God's truth?
- Will we allow fear, doubt, and past experiences to shape our thinking, or will we align with the mind of Christ?

The renewed mind is not just about knowledge—it is about living differently. It is about seeing, thinking, and acting from a place of Kingdom authority. Paul said in Philippians 2:5:

"Let this mind be in you which was also in Christ Jesus." NKJV

This is an invitation—not a command. The mind of Christ is available to us, but we must choose to walk in it.

Reviewing the Keys to a Renewed Mind

Throughout this book, we have explored the power of renewing the mind and how it transforms every aspect of life. Let's briefly review what we have learned:

1. The Power of Right Thinking

- Your thoughts shape your identity and destiny (Proverbs 23:7).
- Transformation happens when you align your mind with God's truth (Romans 12:2).

2. The Word of God as the Foundation for Renewal

- The Bible is the ultimate tool for renewing the mind (Hebrews 4:12).
- Daily meditation on God's Word reshapes our thinking (Joshua 1:8).

3. Kingdom Thinking vs. Carnal Thinking

- A carnal mind leads to fear, doubt, and limitation (Romans 8:5-7).
- A Kingdom mindset sees solutions, abundance, and supernatural possibilities.

4. Aligning with the Mind of Christ

- We already have the mind of Christ (1 Corinthians 2:16).

- A renewed mind sees every situation through Heaven's perspective.

5. Breaking Strongholds and Mental Barriers

- Strongholds are deeply entrenched lies that keep us bound (2 Corinthians 10:3-5).
- We must replace every lie with the truth of God's Word.

6. The Supernatural Power of a Renewed Mind

- A renewed mind unlocks faith, healing, and miracles.
- Jesus thought from Heaven's reality, and so should we.

7. Living from the Reality of Heaven

- We are called to bring Heaven to Earth (Matthew 6:10).
- A renewed mind expects God's supernatural intervention in every area.

8. Transforming Culture Through Renewed Thinking

- A renewed mind influences government, business, education, and media.
- We are called to be lights in the world, transforming culture with Kingdom truth (Matthew 5:14).

9. The Role of Faith in Renewing the Mind

- Faith is the operating system of a renewed mind (Hebrews 11:6).
- A renewed mind sees impossibilities as opportunities for God's power.

10. Walking in Victory as a Lifestyle

- Victory is not a one-time event but a mindset (Romans 8:37).
- A renewed mind does not just experience breakthrough—it sustains it.

Every chapter has been a stepping stone toward a fully renewed mind—a mind that thinks, speaks, and lives from the reality of Heaven.

The Invitation: Will You Live Differently?

Jesus did not come just to show us what God is like—He came to show us how we are meant to live. He walked in:

- Unshakable faith
- Supernatural wisdom
- Kingdom authority
- Absolute confidence in the Father's will

And now He invites us to do the same.

- Will you take responsibility for what you allow to shape your thoughts?
- Will you reject fear, doubt, and worldly thinking and embrace the mind of Christ?
- Will you be the one who brings Kingdom transformation to your family, workplace, and community?

This is your invitation to live a supernatural life, sustained by a renewed mind.

How to Move Forward from Here

To continue growing in mind renewal, I encourage you to take the following action steps:

1. Establish a Daily Renewal Routine

- Read and meditate on God's Word every morning.
- Declare Kingdom truths over yourself daily.

2. Identify and Eliminate Limiting Beliefs

- Ask the Holy Spirit to reveal any strongholds still in your thinking.
- Replace every lie with Scripture-based truth.

3. Speak Only in Agreement with God

- Refuse to speak words of fear, doubt, or negativity.
- Speak only what aligns with Heaven's reality.

4. Surround Yourself with Kingdom-Minded People

- Find people who think and live in faith.
- Stay connected to a community that encourages mind renewal.

5. Act on What You Believe

- Faith is not just believing—it is action (James 2:26).
- Step out and demonstrate the reality of a renewed mind in your everyday life.

Final Words: The Renewed Mind is the Key to Your Destiny

The greatest battles are won in the mind. The level of transformation you experience in your life will be determined by the level of renewal in your thinking. A renewed mind:

- Opens the door to supernatural possibilities.
- Positions you for divine encounters.
- Equips you to fulfill your God-given purpose.

God is calling you higher—to think, live, and operate as Jesus did. The question is:

Will you answer the call?

Your destiny begins in your mind. The choice is yours.

BONUS SECTION:
PRACTICAL ACTIVATION FOR RENEWING THE MIND

Renewing the mind is not just about understanding new concepts—it is about practicing them daily until they become second nature. In this section, you will find practical tools and activations to help you cultivate a transformed mind and maintain Kingdom thinking as a lifestyle.

1. Daily Declarations for Renewing the Mind

Your words shape your reality. The Bible teaches that life and death are in the power of the tongue (Proverbs 18:21). Speaking truth over yourself daily rewires your thinking, strengthens your faith, and aligns your thoughts with God's reality. Below are daily declarations you can speak over yourself to reinforce a renewed mind:

Declarations of Identity:

- I have the mind of Christ, and I think from Heaven's perspective. (1 Corinthians 2:16)
- I am a son/daughter of God, and I live from my Kingdom identity. (Romans 8:15)

- I am not conformed to this world, but I am transformed by the renewing of my mind. (Romans 12:2)

Declarations of Victory:

- I live in victory because I am more than a conqueror in Christ. (Romans 8:37)
- I take every thought captive to the obedience of Christ, and I reject all fear, doubt, and deception. (2 Corinthians 10:5)
- Sin has no power over me, and I walk in righteousness. (Romans 6:14)

Declarations of Faith:

- I walk by faith, not by sight. (2 Corinthians 5:7)
- I expect supernatural breakthroughs in my life. (Mark 9:23)
- All things are possible for me because I believe. (Mark 11:24)

Declarations of Peace and Joy:

- I do not have a spirit of fear, but of power, love, and a sound mind. (2 Timothy 1:7)
- The peace of God guards my heart and mind in Christ Jesus. (Philippians 4:7)
- I have the joy of the Lord, and it is my strength. (Nehemiah 8:10)

Declarations of Kingdom Authority:

- I have been given authority to trample on all the power of the enemy. (Luke 10:19)

- I release Heaven's solutions into every situation I face.
  (Matthew 6:10)
- I bring Kingdom transformation wherever I go.
  (Matthew 5:14)

How to Use These Declarations Daily:

1. Speak them out loud every morning.
2. Personalize them based on your life and challenges.
3. Write new ones based on Scriptures God highlights
   to you.

2. Journaling Exercises for Thought Transformation

Journaling is a powerful tool to process thoughts, track your growth, and partner with the Holy Spirit in renewing your mind. Here are some exercises you can use:

Exercise 1: Identify and Replace Lies with Truth

- Write down any negative or limiting beliefs you have
  about yourself, God, or your circumstances.
- Find Scriptures that contradict those lies and write
  them next to the false belief.
- Pray and declare the truth daily until your thinking
  aligns with it.

Example:

- Lie: "I'm not good enough for God to use me."
- Truth: "I am chosen, and God has good works
  prepared for me to do." (Ephesians 2:10)

Exercise 2: Capture Daily Thoughts

- At the end of each day, write down thoughts that dominated your mind.
- Identify if they were aligned with truth or rooted in fear, doubt, or negativity.
- Ask: "Did I think today as a Kingdom-minded person, or did I conform to worldly thinking?"

Exercise 3: Gratitude and Testimony Journal

- Write down three things you are grateful for every day.
- Document answered prayers and moments of breakthrough.
- Review past entries to see how God has been working in your life.

Exercise 4: Dream with God

- Ask God: "What do You see when You look at me?"
- Journal the visions, words, and impressions He gives you.
- Write down big faith-filled prayers and prophetic words you receive and revisit them regularly.

3. Scripture Meditations for Kingdom Thinking

Meditating on God's Word rewires your mind and helps you think from a Kingdom perspective. Below are key Scriptures for renewing the mind.

Renewing Your Mind

- Romans 12:2 – "Do not be conformed to this world, but be transformed by the renewing of your mind."

- 2 Corinthians 10:5 – "Take every thought captive to the obedience of Christ."

Faith and Expectation

- Hebrews 11:1 – "Faith is the substance of things hoped for, the evidence of things not seen."
- Mark 9:23 – "If you can believe, all things are possible to him who believes."

Victory Over Fear and Anxiety

- 2 Timothy 1:7 – "God has not given us a spirit of fear, but of power, love, and a sound mind."
- Philippians 4:6-7 – "Be anxious for nothing… and the peace of God will guard your hearts and minds."

Kingdom Identity

- 1 Corinthians 2:16 – "We have the mind of Christ."
- Romans 8:15 – "You did not receive the spirit of bondage again to fear, but the Spirit of adoption."

Supernatural Thinking and Authority

- Matthew 6:10 – "Your Kingdom come, Your will be done on earth as it is in heaven."
- Luke 10:19 – "I give you authority… over all the power of the enemy."

How to Meditate on Scripture Daily:

1. Read the verse slowly and repeatedly.
2. Ask the Holy Spirit to give you revelation about it.
3. Write down insights and practical applications.

4. Declare it over your life in prayer.

4. Prayers for Breaking Mental Strongholds

Prayer is essential for shifting mindsets, breaking old thought patterns, and fully embracing Kingdom thinking. Below are powerful prayers to help you demolish strongholds and renew your mind.

Prayer for Breaking Negative Thought Patterns

Father, I surrender my thoughts to You. I repent for any thinking that has been shaped by fear, doubt, or lies. Right now, I take every thought captive to the obedience of Christ. I break agreement with every lie of the enemy, and I replace it with the truth of Your Word. Fill my mind with Your wisdom, and teach me to think like You. In Jesus' name, Amen.

Prayer for Walking in Kingdom Authority

Lord, I thank You that I have the mind of Christ. I refuse to think like a victim—I am a victor in You. I declare that I have authority over fear, doubt, and every negative influence. I choose to live by faith and not by sight. Holy Spirit, lead me in Your ways, and teach me how to think, speak, and act as a Kingdom ambassador. In Jesus' name, Amen.

Prayer for Supernatural Transformation

Heavenly Father, I invite You to transform my mind completely. I reject all worldly thinking and embrace Kingdom thinking. Let my thoughts, words, and actions reflect the reality of Heaven. Renew me daily by Your Spirit and lead me into deeper revelation of who You are and who I am in You. In Jesus' name, Amen.

Final Activation: Your Commitment to a Renewed Mind

Take a moment to reflect:

- What lies have I been believing that I need to break?
- What Kingdom truths do I need to meditate on daily?
- How will I commit to renewing my mind consistently?

Your journey to transformation begins now.

Will you fully embrace the mind of Christ and live from Heaven's reality every day?

The choice is yours.

ABOUT THE AUTHOR

Tom Cornell is the Senior Leader of SOZO Church in Washington state, founder of Walk in the Light International and SOZO Network. Tom is married to his beautiful wife Katy and lives in the Puget Sound area with her and their three kids. He has been in ministry pastoring and teaching the body of Christ since 2008.

He has a passion to see the body of Christ moving from people with an orphan mindset to that of sonship; equipping the body to do the work of Jesus resulting in seeing the Kingdom of God manifested here on earth.